PATHFINDERS
IN EXPLORATION

Exploring Rivers

SCHOOLHOUSE PRESS

Copyright © 1988 by Schoolhouse Press, Inc.
160 Gould Street, Needham
Massachusettes 02194
ISBN 0-8086-1161-5 (hardback)
ISBN 0-8086-1168-2 (paperback)

Original copyright, © Macmillan Education Ltd 1987

Authors: Derek Cullen and John Murray-Robertson

Editorial planning by AMR

Designed and typeset by The Pen and Ink Book Company Ltd, London

Illustrated by Gecko Ltd

Picture research by Faith Perkins

Printed in Hong Kong

88/89/90/91/92/93   6 5 4 3 2 1

Photographic Credits

t=top b=bottom l=left r=right

The author and publishers wish to acknowledge, with thanks, the following photographic sources: 25*l* J. Allan Cash; 25*r* Barnaby's Picture Library, London; 16-17, 17 Bettmann Archive, New York; 10*b*, 12*t* and *b*, 13 Jean-Loup Charmet, Paris; 42*l* and *r* Christina Dodwell; 9*t*, 18*b*, 23, 29, 30*t* and *b*, 32 Mary Evans Picture Library, London; 27 Peter Fraenkel; 20*t*, 22*t*, 24, 31, 33*r* Robert Harding Photograph Library, London; 8, 16, 20*b*, 26*r* Hutchison Photograph Library, London; 15 National Gallery of Washington, Paul Mellon Collection; 22*t* National Portrait Gallery, Scotland; 5*t* and *b*, 10-11, 14, 18*t*, 34, 36, 37*t* and *b*, 38, 39*l* and *r* Peter Newark's Western Americana

Cover photograph courtesy of Picturepoint (UK)

The publishers have made every effort to trace the copyright holders, but if they have inadvertently overlooked any, they will be pleased to make the necessary arrangement at the first opportunity.

Note to the reader
In this book there are some words in the text which are printed in **bold** type. This shows that the word is listed in the glossary on page 46. The glossary gives a brief explanation of words which may be new to you.

Contents

Introduction

The early explorers had no planes, trains, cars, or bikes to take them on their journeys. There were also no good roads in the places they wished to explore. They had to travel on foot or use horses. Often, people used boats because the only way, or **route**, was along the rivers. Traveling by boat was a faster and easier way to travel than going by land. People could also put their stores, or **supplies**, into the boats instead of carrying them.

Sometimes, people traveling by boat were slowed down or held up. If they were traveling up the river, the flow of the water, or the **current**, ran against them. Often, in steep parts of the river, the water rushed down very fast and this fast water, or **rapids**, blocked their way. They had to unload their boats and carry them to calmer water. In colder lands, people had to travel where there was a lot of ice and snow. They were often not prepared for the very cold conditions.

▲ These people live by the Xingu River in Brazil. They hunt for fish in the river and animals in the forest. They use canoes hollowed out of tree trunks to travel along the river. The Xingu River leads into the Amazon River.

We shall see in this book that rivers were more than just a "highway" for explorers. Some people wanted to find where a river started from, or its **source**. These people explored rivers like the Amazon in South America and the Niger in Africa. Above all, there was the search for the source of the Nile River. People knew the river flowed through Egypt and emptied into the Mediterranean Sea, but where did it begin? The search for its source led to many adventures for over a hundred years.

The Search for Gold and Spices

Four hundred years ago, the Spanish ruled the area in South America now called Peru. At that time, two Spaniards, called Francisco de Orellana and Gonzalo Pizarro, went on a long journey, or an **expedition**, down the Amazon River. They were looking for a city called El Dorado, which means City of Gold. The city had been mentioned in old stories. They also wanted to find the Lands of **Cinnamon**. This spice was highly valued at that time.

The Expedition Begins

The Spaniards built a boat called the *San Pedro*. They started sailing high in the Andes Mountains and followed the Coca River. Then, food became very short. Pizarro sent Orellana with fifty-seven men in the boat to find food. The boat did not return. Pizarro and the rest of the men decided to go back to their base in Quito, Peru. Only a few of the men got back safely with Pizarro. Most of the men died of hunger or fever on the way.

▲ This map of South America was made in 1582, forty years after Francisco de Orellana traveled along the Amazon River. The Amazon is the second longest river in the world. It is 4,063 miles long. It has many tributaries and begins in the Andes Mountains. The river flows east across South America and into the Atlantic Ocean. The Amazon is 150 miles wide when it flows into the Atlantic.

▶ In the 1500's, the Spanish wanted to find gold and spices in the unexplored land of South America. The Spanish soldiers fought the Inca people and became their rulers.

Down the Amazon

Orellana and his men could not return with the boat to Pizarro. The river had a strong current and they could not turn back. Also, they could not find any food. After some time, the boat entered the Napo River. This river later joins the Amazon.

Among the men, or **crew** of the boat, there was a priest named Gaspar de Carvajal. He wrote an account of their journey down the Amazon, which is how we know what happened to them. At first, their main worry was the lack of food. They tried digging up roots in the forest. They even boiled their leather belts and shoes and ate them with **herbs**. The herbs provided the flavor.

The *Victoria*

The crew of the *San Pedro* knew that they could not turn back. They also had no idea of what lay ahead. They knew that they were on a big river. At any moment, they might be faced with death. They were attacked by insects. In the rushing waters below, lay deadly meat-eating piranha fish. On the sides, or **banks**, of the river there was thick green jungle. When they reached any village, they were afraid they might meet unfriendly, or **hostile**, people. The Spaniards tried to make friends with the people to obtain food. For the first part of their journey, the native people helped them and allowed them to go on their way safely.

▲ The forest along the Amazon River is very thick. Orellana's men were afraid to stray far from the river. They might have gotten lost or been attacked.

The Amazon River was so wide that Orellana soon thought he must be near the Atlantic Ocean. He decided to build another boat which could sail on the sea. This was not easy to do in the middle of the jungle with few tools. It took two months to build the *Victoria*, which was the name of their new boat.

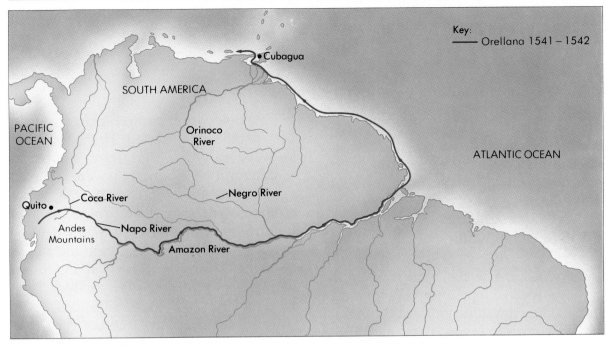

▲ Francisco de Orellana's route down the
Amazon River.

The First Battle

The men set off again with the *San
Pedro* and the *Victoria*. They were
attacked by the native people. These
people beat drums, blew wooden
trumpets, and yelled loudly. They also
carried **blowpipes** and poison-tipped
arrows. The Spaniards landed and built a
fort to protect themselves. They raided a
nearby village for food, but ten men were
cut off by 2,000 tribesmen. The rest of the
men came to the rescue and saved them.
They took to their boats once more, and
sailed off downstream. The tribesmen
still came after them in their canoes. The
Spaniards could not stop or land for
hundreds of miles. By this time, eighteen
Spaniards had been wounded, but only
one had been killed. It could have been
much worse.

▲ The people who lived around the Amazon
River used blowpipes. A poison-tipped dart was
blown out of the pipe at the animals they were
hunting. The blowpipes were made of wood. This
man is carving a mouthpiece for a blowpipe.

7

The Journey Continues

At last, Orellana and his men found a village where the people were more friendly. They stayed there for three days and ate as much as they could. They also stocked their boats with salted meat. The meat was salted to stop it from going bad in the heat.

The forest grew like thick walls along the banks of the Amazon River. Sometimes, the walls were broken by paths or even large highways made of stone. The crew did not dare to wander too far from their boats. They were afraid people might attack them or cut off their return to the river. Both banks of the river seemed full of hidden dangers.

They passed the **junction** of the Amazon where it joins up with the wide Negro River. The waters of the Negro are "black as ink." This color comes from the mud carried down 1,200 miles from the high mountains.

The Amazons

The Spaniards passed places where very hostile people lived. The men had to be very careful when they landed to search for food. Soon, they were attacked again. This time, it was by tall white women with long hair. These women fought very bravely. They seemed to be much stronger than their menfolk. When people in Europe heard about these women, they became very excited. They thought a mythological tribe, called the Amazons, had been found. The river along which the women lived was called the Amazon because of this story.

Journey's End

The Spaniards escaped from these women and hurried downstream. The boats had arrows stuck into their sides. They were attacked yet again. This time, the priest was wounded in the eye. In

◄ The Negro River is a tributary of the Amazon. It gets its name from the fine black soil which is washed into the river by heavy rains. The soil makes the water look black. "Negro" is the Spanish word for "black."

▲ Some of Orellana's battles were with the Amazon women. These women were warriors, and they were very white skinned and tall. Their hair was very long, and often they wore it wound around their heads.

spite of the pain, he kept on writing the story of their journey. Some of the crew were killed by the poison-tipped arrows.

At last, they reached the ocean. Even there, their troubles were not over. Their small boats were tossed by the ocean waves. Then, they reached Nueva Cadiz, a port on the island of Cubagua. This was a Spanish port near the **mouth** of the Orinoco River where it empties into the Atlantic Ocean. They were safe at long last.

It had been a long journey. The men had made no plans for the two year expedition. They had found no gold or spices, but they were the first to cross the South American **continent**. They had also been the first people to explore the Amazon River.

▲ Francisco de Orellana was born in Trujillo, Spain. The people there have built a statue to remember the first European to travel down the Amazon.

A New Route to Asia

Over 400 years ago, people in Europe wanted to find a new sea route to Asia, or the **East**, as it was called. These lands grew many spices which were very valuable in Europe at that time. Spain and Portugal had found a route around the Cape of Good Hope, at the southern tip of Africa. This route was long and the seas were very rough. The French king wanted to find his own sea route. He thought there would be a northern route from the Atlantic Ocean to the Pacific Ocean.

In 1533, a French pirate named Jacques Cartier asked the king of France to send him to search for this new sea route to Asia. King Francis agreed. In 1534, Cartier set off for North America with two small ships and 120 men. He was to look for the **Northwest Passage**.

After the long voyage across the Atlantic, Cartier reached Newfoundland. There, the native people told Cartier of a wide river. He took two of the native people with him and sailed to the river's mouth. Then, he returned to France to tell King Francis about what he had found.

The St. Lawrence River

King Francis believed that this river could be the Northwest Passage. Cartier set off again, this time with three ships. When he sailed into the mouth of the

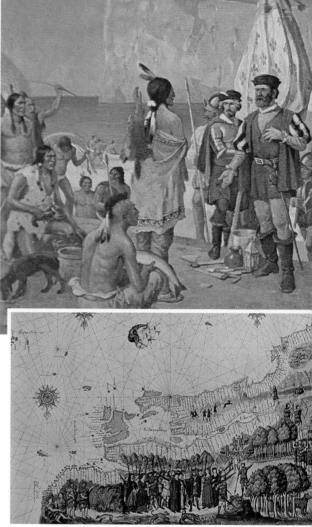

Jacques Cartier sailed from France to Canada in 1534. He landed on the Gaspé Peninsular near the Percé Rock. The people there told him about the St. Lawrence River.

river, it was the feast day of St. Lawrence. Cartier gave this saint's name to the river. He sailed up the St. Lawrence River to a place near the **site** of the present-day city of Quebec. There, he met some native people of the Huron tribe. The Hurons called this part of the river "Canada." They tried to frighten away the French by dressing up as devils. They wore dog skins and put horns on their heads.

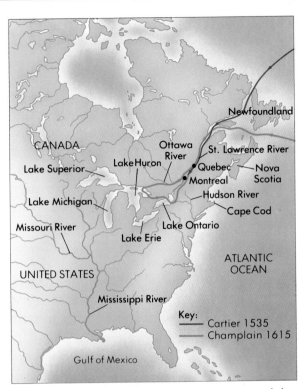

◀ This map was drawn by a Portuguese mapmaker about 1547. If you turn the book upside down, you will see the Gulf of St. Lawrence. The map shows Jacques Cartier arriving in Canada with French settlers.

▲ Jacques Cartier explored the area around the St. Lawrence River in the 1530's and 1540's. He was looking for the Northwest Passage. Although he did not find the route through to the Pacific Ocean, he did find out a lot about North America. Samuel de Champlain went farther down the St. Lawrence, and reached the Great Lakes in 1615.

Stopped by the Rapids

Cartier sailed on farther up the river. The native people thought Cartier was a god who could heal the sick. Cartier climbed a nearby hill which he called "Mont Real," which means "royal mountain." The city of Montreal stands on this site today.

From the top of the hill, Cartier could see a long way into the distance. He could see more rivers and rapids, and he was told of many other rapids beyond. There was no sign of the sea. He knew this could not be the Northwest Passage.

Cartier had a hard journey back. He had to spend the winter on the river bank. He and his men suffered from disease. They were saved by native people who gave them their own medicines and food.

Cartier could not know what his voyage had meant. He had opened the way for the French to settle in North America. The St. Lawrence River was to become a great seaway into the heart of the continent.

Success for the French

Some French people came to North America and settled in the area Cartier had explored. Many of them came to hunt animals for furs. No one tried to go farther west for over seventy years. Then, in 1603, another French explorer named Samuel de Champlain followed Cartier's route up the St. Lawrence.

Champlain learned from the Indians about a huge **waterfall** in the area to the south where the river fell over a very high cliff. We now know that they meant the mighty Niagara Falls. Champlain began to make maps of the whole area.

The next year, Champlain came back to the coast of Nova Scotia. The freezing winter months killed many of his crew, but Champlain continued with his work. He made a map of a large part of the northeast coastline from Nova Scotia to Cape Cod.

New France

In 1608, Champlain built three small huts on the banks of the St. Lawrence. He also built a **warehouse** to store his furs in. This site was to become the city of Quebec. He still felt that somewhere off the St. Lawrence River, there was a route to the Pacific Ocean and to Asia. He spent the rest of his life trying to find it. More French people began to settle in "New France." Samuel de Champlain became known as the Father of French Canada.

▲ The Niagara Falls are on a section of the Niagara River between Lake Ontario and Lake Erie. An island divides the Falls into two. The American Falls are 163 feet high and the Horseshoe Falls are 153 feet high.

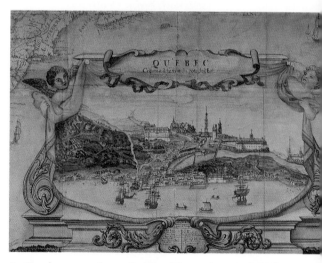

▲ Quebec was founded by Champlain in 1608. For many years, it was only a base for fur traders. By the time this picture was painted in 1700, Quebec had grown to be a town.

The French became friendly with the Huron tribe. Champlain helped them fight other American Indian people called the Iroquois. They were enemies of the Hurons. Champlain killed two of their chiefs. From then on, the Iroquois became the enemies of the French, too.

▲ The Iroquois were Native Americans who lived between the Hudson River and the St. Lawrence and Lake Erie. The Iroquois often attacked the French explorers in the 1600's

The Great Lakes

Champlain and his men began to explore the valley of the Ottawa River. They found a new route through to Lake Huron, one of the Great Lakes. They paddled their canoes into Lake Ontario. Champlain was wounded twice in a battle with the Iroquois, and had to be carried on a stretcher. He and his men could not go straight back by the St. Lawrence. They had to go back to Quebec in a huge circle in order to avoid the Iroquois.

Champlain was not able to leave Quebec again, so he sent a man called Etienne Brulé to explore farther. Brulé was the first person from Europe to reach the far side of Lake Superior.

Another of Champlain's men paddled down Lake Michigan and landed on the other side. He thought he had reached Asia, or the **Orient**, and put on a Chinese robe. Champlain had given him this to impress the people of the Orient. Imagine his surprise when he found American Indians. They must have been just as surprised!

Champlain died in 1635. During his lifetime, he had opened up new areas of land for the French. More French people came to settle in the areas Champlain had mapped. It was the beginning of French Canada.

Robert Cavelier de La Salle

▲ Louis Joliet and Father Jacques Marquette in 1673 became the first Europeans to travel along the Mississippi River.

The French still wanted to find a new sea route to Asia. They heard of a wide river flowing south from the Great Lakes. This was the Mississippi River. Perhaps this river might take them to the Pacific Ocean and on to Asia. A fur trader named Louis Joliet went down the Mississippi and reached the point where the river joins the Missouri.

The *Griffon*

Another French explorer heard of the Mississippi. His name was Robert Cavelier de La Salle. In 1666, he had set out from France to make his fortune in North America. He became a fur trader. In 1669, he set out to explore the rivers and the lakes. He found the Ohio River and explored lands south of the Great Lakes. He decided to build a ship to carry his furs across the Great Lakes. He could use this ship to increase his trade. La Salle could not build the ship on the St. Lawrence because it would not be possible to get it past Niagara Falls. La Salle and his friends built their ship, the *Griffon*, by the Great Lakes. While they were building the ship, they were often attacked by the Iroquois. When the ship was finished, it weighed about fifty-five tons, and the sails were made from deerskins. The native people called it "the winged canoe."

Fort Heartbreak

La Salle dreamed of a large number of ships, or a **fleet**, which could be used for his fur trade. He also wanted to explore the rivers and find a route to the sea. He could not take the *Griffon* down the rivers because the ship was too big. La Salle and his men sent the *Griffon* back to Niagara and set off on their journey using canoes. They crossed the Great Lakes to the south of Lake Michigan. Their food ran low and they almost starved. There was no game to hunt. Once, La Salle and his men found a buffalo, or bison. This gave them something to eat and saved their lives. The weather was very cold. The men wore soft leather shoes, called **moccasins**. They slept in these at night to keep their feet from frostbite.

La Salle then crossed overland to the Illinois River. He built a **fort** there. It had been such a bad journey that he called it Fort Heartbreak.

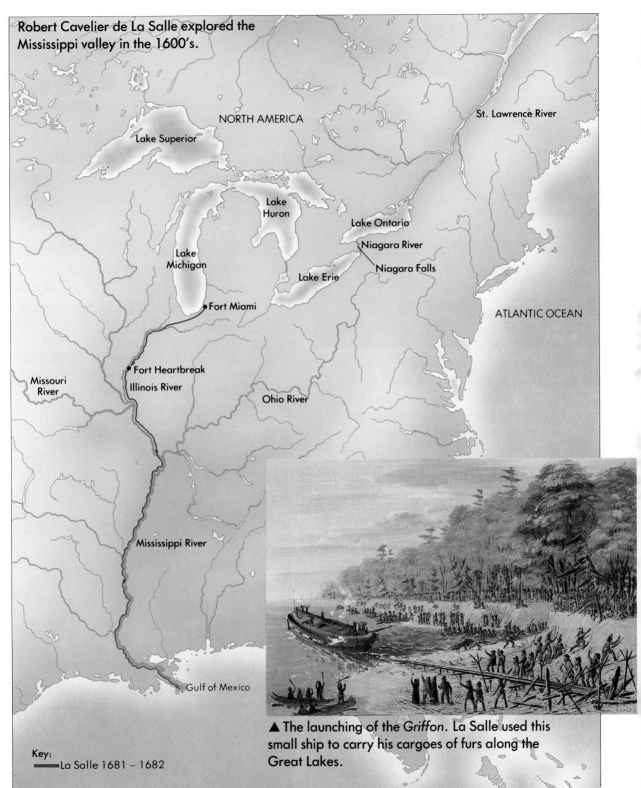

Robert Cavelier de La Salle explored the Mississippi valley in the 1600's.

NORTH AMERICA

St. Lawrence River

Lake Superior

Lake Huron

Lake Ontario

Niagara River

Niagara Falls

Lake Michigan

Lake Erie

Fort Miami

ATLANTIC OCEAN

Fort Heartbreak

Missouri River

Illinois River

Ohio River

Mississippi River

Gulf of Mexico

Key:
La Salle 1681 – 1682

▲ The launching of the *Griffon*. La Salle used this small ship to carry his cargoes of furs along the Great Lakes.

15

The loss of the *Griffon*

▲ Lake Michigan is the sixth largest lake in the world. It is one of the Great Lakes in North America. The others are Lake Superior, Lake Huron, Lake Erie, and Lake Ontario. Today, they are an important inland waterway. The lakes are linked to the Atlantic Ocean by the St. Lawrence Seaway.

La Salle went back to Niagara by canoe with seven men. He left one of his men, Henry de Tonty, in charge of a group, or **party**, of men at Fort Heartbreak. La Salle kept hoping to find the *Griffon* on Lake Michigan. He learned later that it had sunk, and its crew had all drowned. La Salle and his men nearly died, too, on the 1,000-mile journey. There was too much ice on the lake, and they had to leave their canoes behind. They had to walk waist high in mud and freezing water. Sometimes, they slept in trees because there was no dry ground. When they reached Niagara after sixty-five days, they were all very sick.

Trouble at Fort Heartbreak

Back at Fort Heartbreak, the men were very unhappy. They had heard from the Indian people about the loss of the *Griffon*. La Salle owed them money. The weather was bad, and they were attacked by the Iroquois in the area. The men took up arms against de Tonty and **mutinied**. De Tonty and a few loyal men ran away into the forest. There, they were captured by the Iroquois.

A few weeks later, La Salle heard of the mutiny. He hurried back to the fort. The men who were not loyal to him had gone before he arrived. There was also no sign of de Tonty.

▼ Louis Hennepin explored the Great Lakes with La Salle. Hennepin was captured by the Sioux. While traveling with them, he visited these Falls which he named the Falls of St. Anthony.

After several months, the Iroquois let de Tonty and his men go free. The Frenchmen were so weak by this time that the Iroquois thought they would die. However, another tribe came to their rescue. They gave them food and de Tonty's group managed to get back safely to Fort Heartbreak.

Down the Mississippi

La Salle tried to find de Tonty and failed. Then, he went back to Fort Miami, a French fort, on Lake Michigan. In December, 1681, La Salle was able to begin his life's dream. He set out from Fort Miami to find the famous Northwest Passage route to Asia. He started his journey by going down the Mississippi to the sea. He took with him twenty-three Frenchmen and about the same number of American Indian people.

The men set off in the winter. They put their supplies on sleds and made their way on top of the frozen river. When the ice melted, they went along the river in their canoes. The Indian people they met were friendly, and there were many deer and fish to eat.

At last, La Salle reached the mouth of the river. There, it split into three small rivers. The men went in three groups to explore the different **channels**. On April 9, 1682, La Salle sailed out into the Gulf of Mexico. He was the first European to travel the length of the Mississippi. The journey had taken four months. La Salle named the country around the river's mouth "Louisiana" after his King, Louis XIV of France. La Salle returned to France where he became a hero. He later returned to America where he died in Texas on March 19, 1687.

▲ La Salle and de Tonty went down the Mississippi River by canoe. When they reached the mouth of the river, they claimed the area for France. They named it Louisiana after their King, Louis XIV.

Exploring the Niger

▲ Timbuktu is a city on the Niger River. It had been an important city for desert traders for hundreds of years. Until the 1820's, Timbuktu had not been seen by any European.

About 200 years ago, people from Europe did not know very much about the central parts, or **interior**, of West Africa. Some Arabs had traveled in the area. There was talk of a city called Timbuktu, and a big river called the Niger.

The mouth of the Niger River is marshy and splits into many channels. People did not realize that these small channels were the mouth of a river that was 2,000 miles in length. No one knew the source of this river. They did not realize that it was the same river spoken of in the stories.

In 1788, a special group of people called the African Association was

▲ Mungo Park was twenty-four years old when he arrived in Africa. He wanted to learn about the people of Africa and their way of life. Later, he wrote about his travels in Africa.

formed in London. Its aim was to find out about the Niger. The person who helped most to explore this river was a man named Mungo Park.

The Ship's Doctor

Mungo Park was a Scottish doctor. For a time, he became a ship's surgeon, but his great wish was to explore. He went to see the African Association because he wanted to try to find the Niger. He knew that three people had already died in the attempt. Park knew nothing about exploring. He was ready to learn as he went along.

When Park first arrived in Africa, he stayed at a British fort on the Gambia River. However, before he could set out, he caught a fever. Park had to wait six months before he was well again. Then in 1795, he set out to follow the Gambia River inland. He went with two **slave traders**. These people bought and sold slaves. Park also had four other men with him. They had only two days supply of food, but had brought along beads and tobacco to trade with the native people. Soon, the other men left Park, and he continued his journey with only two servants. The servants told him it was crazy to go any farther. Park would not listen. He sent one servant back with his diary which described his journey so far, and continued with the other servant.

The Prisoner

Park crossed from the Gambia River to the Senegal River. He then headed across the **savanna**, which is a grassy area south of the Sahara Desert. It was very hot, and Park and his servant had to worry about finding food.

When Park got near the Niger, he found that a local ruler was getting ready for war. This ruler told Park to go north to avoid the fighting. Park and his servant went off into the dry **bushland**. They had very little water with them. When they had almost reached the Niger, they were taken prisoner by a man named Chief Ali. Ali took all of Park's supplies, except his **compass**. This was very valuable to him, because he needed a compass to show him which direction he was going in.

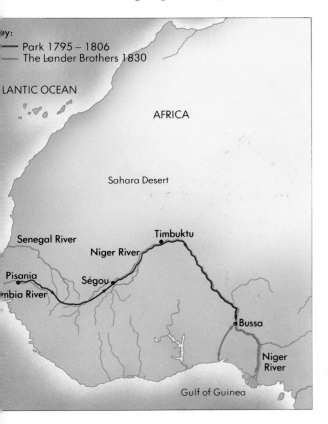

Key:
— Park 1795 – 1806
— The Lander Brothers 1830

ATLANTIC OCEAN

AFRICA

Sahara Desert

Timbuktu

Senegal River

Niger River

Pisania

Ségou

Gambia River

Bussa

Niger River

Gulf of Guinea

◀ The journeys of discovery made by Mungo Park and the Lander brothers in Northwest Africa. The course of the Niger River was a great mystery to explorers in the 1700's and 1800's. Mungo Park traveled down the river most of the way. The journey was completed by Richard and John Lander in 1830.

Escape

While Park was held prisoner, he became sick with fever again. Sometimes, he thought it would be better to die, but his will to live was strong. At last, Park had a chance to escape from Chief Ali. He was able to get a horse and ride away. He had no food or water with him, and he became too weak to continue. He lay on the sand, dying. Then, a light rain fell. Park found the strength to carry on. Some native people took pity on him and gave him food and grain for his horse. Then, at last, Park reached the banks of the Niger River.

Return to the Gambia

Park had reached the upper parts, or **reaches**, of the Niger. He planned to follow the river to find where it flowed into the sea. He made one trip downstream, but was unable to reach Timbuktu. Park knew now he could not go on without help. He wrote in his diary that he was worn down by sickness. He had to go back to the British fort on the Gambia River. It was a long and slow journey back.

When Park reached the fort, people were shocked to see him. They thought he had died. He felt he had failed, but people treated him like a hero. Park returned to Britain where he got married. His account of his travels became a best-selling book in Britain. He stayed in Britain for five years, but the wish to explore was in his blood.

▲ The Niger River is 2,614 miles long, and curves through West Africa. It is the third longest river in Africa. It empties into the Gulf of Guinea.

◀ In Mungo Park's time, the people who lived beside the Niger River used boats made of a water plant called papyrus. The young man in the picture is using a papyrus boat.

Back to the Niger

In 1805, Park set out for the Niger again. This time he went with thirty-eight soldiers. He was also given £5,000. With this money, he bought goods to trade with the native people.

The journey to the Niger was very bad again. Only a handful of men reached the river. There, they built a boat which was forty-two feet long, from two canoes. They called it the *Joliba* after the local name for the river. Park and his men began their journey downstream. They were not sure where the river would take them.

The goods for trading that Park had brought with him ran out. The local chiefs grew hostile. Park and his men were attacked near a place called Bussa. They had to abandon the *Joliba*, and Park was drowned. This was in January, 1806. Park left written accounts of his 940-mile journey down the Niger River. These accounts showed that the river turned south towards the Atlantic Ocean.

It was not until 1830 that the riddle of the Niger was solved. The Lander brothers paddled the last part of the Niger River into the Gulf of Guinea.

▼ Richard Lander and his brother John at Badgary in Nigeria. In 1830, they traveled down the Niger River by canoe. They started from Bussa in Nigeria and completed the journey to the mouth of the river.

The Riddle of the Nile

On the eastern side of Africa, there was an even greater riddle to solve than that of the Niger. People wanted to find the source of the longest and most famous of all rivers, the Nile. The Egyptians had lived along the banks of this river for thousands of years, but no one knew where its source was. The riddle was even greater because the river split into two parts. One part was called the White Nile and the other part was called the Blue Nile. The city of Khartoum stands where the Blue Nile joins the White Nile.

James Bruce

A Scottish man named James Bruce wanted to try to solve the riddle. He wanted to find the source of the Blue Nile. He was strong and tough. He had been married, but his wife had died after only one year. He was good at learning languages. He knew some Arabic, and even some Amharic and Ge'ez. These are two of the languages spoken in Ethiopia. He loved to travel and also had great charm.

In 1768, Bruce went to Egypt, and then started to sail up the Nile. Farther up the river, he joined a group of people who were crossing overland with camels.

▶ James Bruce's journeys in Abyssinia in the 1700's. The country is now called Ethiopia. Bruce was looking for the source of the Nile.

A group such as this is called a **caravan**. Bruce reached Massawa on the Red Sea in September, 1769. He was at the gateway to Ethiopia.

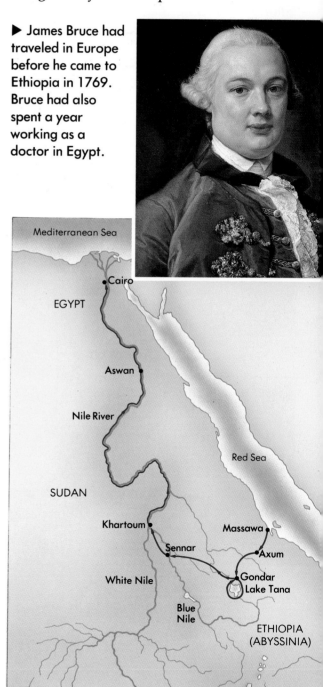

▶ James Bruce had traveled in Europe before he came to Ethiopia in 1769. Bruce had also spent a year working as a doctor in Egypt.

▶ Gondar was the ancient capital city of Ethiopia. Most of the people lived in small round houses made from the local clay. The Emperor's palace was a large stone building which was surrounded by a high wall. Bruce became friendly with Ras Mikael, who lived in the Emperor's palace.

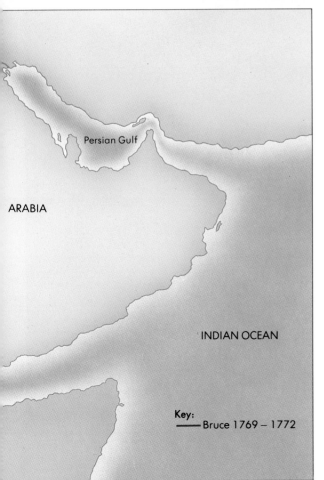

Persian Gulf

ARABIA

INDIAN OCEAN

Key:
—— Bruce 1769 – 1772

Journey into Ethiopia

Bruce started his journey by climbing into the highlands from the coast. Then, he headed for Gondar, the ancient capital city. On his journey, Bruce wrote about the life and customs of the people of Ethiopia. His book was called *Travels to Discover the Source of the Nile*.

Bruce took a **quadrant** with him to measure the height of the sun or stars. It would help him to give the exact position of the source of the Blue Nile when he found it. The quadrant was so heavy it took two teams of four men to carry it.

Bruce found Ethiopia in a state of war. One ruler had just been murdered. His **heir** was only fifteen years old. The man who had the most power at that time was Ras Mikael, Prince of Tigre. Bruce made sure he became friendly with Ras Mikael.

23

The Source of the Blue Nile

Bruce was well liked in Ras Mikael's court. The ladies liked to talk to him, and he allowed them to cut his hair in "the Amharic fashion." He was also a very good horseman and used to ride over the steep countryside with Ras Mikael and his friends. But, Bruce could not forget his main purpose. He wanted to find the source of the Blue Nile.

▼ The Blue Nile passes through deep valleys as it flows through the highlands of Ethiopia.

Bruce asked Ras Mikael if he could travel through the part of the country which contained the Blue Nile. In October, 1770, he started up the river. He found that it became smaller and smaller. He came to a place where water rushed out of the earth. Bruce said it was "pure and **limpid**." The water was very clear. Bruce was very happy because he thought he was the first European to find the source of the Nile. It was proved later that some **missionaries** from Europe had seen the springs before Bruce. Also, the "true" Nile was really the White Nile, not the Blue Nile. The source of the true Nile was still to be found.

Bruce Returns to the Court

Bruce went back to Ras Mikael's court. There, he was shocked by the cruelty of the war. When Ras Mikael lost the war, Bruce felt that the time had come for him to go home. He had been in Ethiopia for over two years. He decided to travel back overland following the Nile. It took Bruce one year more to reach Cairo in Egypt, 2,000 miles to the north.

▼ The Tisisat Falls near the source of the Blue Nile in Ethiopia.

▶ James Bruce in the highlands of Ethiopia during his journey.

Down the Nile to Cairo

Bruce saw many things on his long journey back to Cairo. In the Sudan, he helped to cure a local ruler who was sick. The ruler then wanted him to stay and marry one of his daughters. In the end, Bruce got away by drawing his gun on the ruler. Bruce continued to Sennar. There, he saw the famous Black Horse of Sennar. This was an army of soldiers who rode horses. Bruce said their horses were superb. The people of Sennar kept Bruce a prisoner for four months. At last, he managed to escape and crossed 350 miles of desert. In November, 1772, he arrived in Aswan. He was barefoot, and almost dying of thirst. When Bruce reached Cairo, he had been away from Europe for almost four years.

The True Source

In 1856, Richard Burton and John Speke were chosen by a group of people in London to look for the true source of the Nile. Both men had served in the British Army in India for many years.

▼ Richard Burton grew up in Europe. He traveled to many countries and could speak twenty-five languages. He wrote books about his travels and about life in the countries he visited. Here he is dressed in Arab clothing. He spent many years in Arab countries.

▶ Zanzibar is an island off the east coast of Africa. In the 1800's, it was an important trading centre for ivory and spices.

The two men did not try to follow the Nile upstream from Egypt as other explorers had done. They went inland from the coast of East Africa. Burton and Speke were going to look for the "Mountains of the Moon" which people had told them about. Could these mountains be the source of the Nile?

The Great Lakes

In 1857, Burton and Speke set off from an island off the coast of East Africa called Zanzibar. This was a busy port at the time, and the two men could easily pick up supplies there. The journey inland from the coast proved to be very difficult. Burton and Speke crossed flooded rivers and marshes. They also had to cut their way through forests. On the way, many of the porters who were carrying their supplies ran away. Food became very scarce. Still, Burton and Speke continued, but they were both very sick. Burton could no longer walk. Speke became deaf and blind.

After seven months, Burton and Speke reached Lake Tanganyika. They were the first people from Europe to see it. They hoped this was the source of the Nile. The two men sailed north on the lake to see if this was the true source. They were looking for a river flowing north which could be the Nile. All the rivers were flowing into the lake from the south. Sadly, this proved that the lake could not be the source of the Nile.

On the way back, Speke left Burton, and set off to find another great lake he had heard about. Speke reached the southern part of Lake Victoria. There, he found a river flowing westwards. He was sure he had found the source of the Nile at last.

The Quarrel

Speke joined Burton again. Burton would not accept Speke's claim to have found the source of the Nile. Burton said they should both go to Lake Victoria, so that he could check the river for himself. In the end, neither of them could go because they were too sick.

The two men agreed to say nothing about their travels until they were both back in Britain. Speke returned to Britain before Burton, and he told people he had found the source of the Nile. Speke became famous because of his story. Burton was very angry with Speke because he had broken his promise.

▼ Lake Victoria was visited by many explorers in the 1800's.

Journey to Lake Victoria

▲ John Speke always wrote down the details of his travels and the things he saw. Speke and Grant also drew the first map of Lake Victoria.

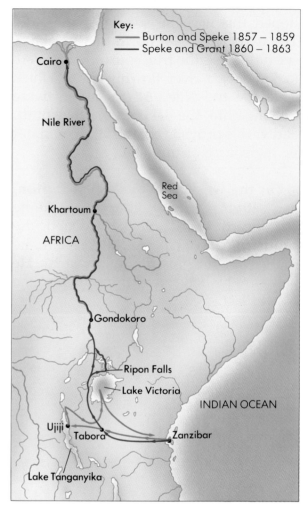

▲ The journeys of discovery of Burton, Speke, and Grant in the 1800's. Burton and Speke were the first Europeans to see Lake Tanganyika. Speke returned on a later journey with James Grant and discovered that Lake Victoria was the source of the Nile. People still did not believe that this lake was the true source. The search continued for many years.

In 1860, Speke was sent back to East Africa in order to prove his claim. This time, he went with a man named James Grant. Speke wanted to explore the north of Lake Victoria and then to follow the Nile through Sudan and Egypt to the sea. He planned to have boats waiting for him at Gondokoro on the Nile in Sudan.

Speke's journey did not go as well as he had planned. Over half of the porters who had come with him ran away. He ran short of food and supplies. When Speke and Grant got near Lake Victoria, they found a lot of fighting going on between the people there. Both men became sick. Grant could not walk. He had to stay in one village for four months to get better. There, he was robbed while Speke was away hunting for food.

It was now more than a year since the two men had set out on their journey. They had very little food left, and only one of their mules was still alive.

The Source of the Nile

Grant recovered from his sickness, and both men made their way around Lake Victoria. Sometimes, they had to stay with local chiefs. Some were friendly, but others could be cruel and hostile. One chief, named Mutesa, kept Speke and Grant prisoner for five months.

At last, Speke was able to get away. He went alone to find a waterfall known as The Stones. It was a big outlet of water from Lake Victoria. The water fell almost thirteen feet over steep rocks before it rushed away towards the north. Speke was sure he was standing at the source of the Nile. If he were, the river should go to Gondokoro.

▼ Speke and Grant had been traveling for many months when they reached Gondokoro. There, they met Florence and Samuel Baker, who were on their way to Lake Victoria.

The Journey Home

Speke was joined by Grant, and both men made their way down the river. They had to leave their canoes behind when they met rapids. Then, they had to walk through grass which was ten feet high. The grass was sharp and cut their clothes and skin. At last, Speke and Grant reached Gondokoro. The riddle was solved at last. At Gondokoro, they met a couple from Britain named Samuel and Florence Baker. These two people gave Speke and Grant food and supplies for their return journey to Cairo.

Speke and Grant came back to Britain. Burton and his friends still did not believe that Speke had found the source of the Nile. In 1864, a meeting between Burton and Speke was set up. Speke never arrived. He had been killed the day before the meeting in a hunting accident. No one could explain how it had really happened.

The Bakers in Africa

Samuel Baker was British. He met his wife in Europe while he was building a railroad there. Her name was Florence and she was Hungarian. Samuel Baker was thirty-eight years old then, and he planned to be an explorer. Florence decided to join him on his travels.

The Bakers spent a year learning Arabic and getting to know North Africa. They learned how to hunt. At last, they felt that they were ready. In 1862, the Bakers left Khartoum in Sudan for Gondokoro, which was 1,000 miles to the south. They sailed up the Nile with three boats.

The Bakers soon found that the river became marshy and choked with tall grassy plants, called **reeds**. The boats had to be pulled by ropes from the shore.

▲ Florence and Samuel Baker explored tributaries of the Nile before they set off to find its source. In the desert regions, they often traveled by camel.

The King of Bunyoro

The Bakers arrived in Gondokoro at last. It was there that they met Speke and Grant. They stayed in the town for a short time and then headed south again. They wanted to explore more of Lake Victoria, and they also wanted to find out if another lake fed into it.

▼ Kamrasi, King of Bunyoro, was a local ruler in East Africa. He demanded gifts from any European who passed through his land.

Both the Bakers became sick. Then, they met the King of Bunyoro who took all of their belongings. The King took Samuel Baker's compass, watch and rifle. The King also wanted to take Florence away, but Baker drew his pistol. After that, the King let them go.

▲ The Nile flows into Lake Albert over the Murchison Falls. The Falls were named after Sir Roderick Murchison, President of the Royal Geographical Society. The Society helped many explorers to travel by giving them money for their expeditions to Africa.

Lake Albert

The Bakers' horses had all died, and the couple had to use oxen to carry their supplies. Speke had given them maps, but these maps did not show how hard the country was to travel through. Once, Florence nearly drowned in soft mud. She was very sick for two days. Samuel was sure that she would die.

When Florence was better, the Bakers moved on. They found another big lake and called it Lake Albert after Queen Victoria's husband. They found that the Nile flowed into the lake down the 130 feet high Murchison Falls. They thought Lake Albert might also be another source of the Nile. Now, we know this is not the case. The Nile flows in and then out of the same end of Lake Albert.

31

Around Lake Albert

The Bakers hired canoes and oarsmen so they could explore Lake Albert. First, the people they had hired to row their boats ran away. Then, there was a sudden storm and the lake became very rough. The Bakers made some **rudders** to steer the boat with, and Samuel made his cloak into a sail.

The area around the lake was deserted because of the fighting going on between the native people. The Bakers could not find food. They could find no one to help hem get back to Gondokoro. They had to eat bad grain which they found in an empty village. Then, they had another attack of fever. They were both so sick that they had to lie on the floor of a hut near the lake. The King of Bunyoro would not help them. He wanted gifts from them which they could not give him. He was now their enemy. It seemed as if they would never be able to get home to tell people about the lake they had found.

▼ Expeditions relied on local guides and others to help carry their food and equipment. Many of Florence and Samuel Baker's helpers left them when they reached Lake Albert.

Rescue

A trader named Ibrahim was passing through the area. He had met the Bakers before on their journey towards Lake Albert. He said he would help them and take them back north. There were over a 1,000 men with Ibrahim. They were carrying the trader's goods. When they reached Gondokoro, the Bakers were very happy. They rode ahead to the little town, firing their guns to tell of their return. No one was there to greet them. Their friends had gone away, thinking the Bakers were dead. It was two years since they had left.

The Journey Back

There was only one hope of reaching Khartoum. One boat had been left at Gondokoro. The sailors who had used it had died of a disease called the **plague**. The Bakers bought the boat and scrubbed it clean. They also burned tobacco leaves which they thought would help to kill the germs. Then, they set sail with a new crew. On May 5, 1865, they reached Khartoum in this boat, but some of the crew caught the plague and died. The Bakers continued down the Nile River and arrived safely in Cairo five months later. They had been away for over four years.

▶ Samuel Baker learned to hunt animals as a young man. In Africa, he hunted elephants, rhinos and hippos.

◀ Samuel and Florence Baker arrived in Gondokoro in 1863. Gondokoro was a small town used by ivory traders. Boats carrying ivory went down the Nile from this town to the coast. Often, explorers used Gondokoro as a base.

Stanley Explores Africa

Henry Stanley is often thought of as the man who found the famous David Livingstone in Africa. Stanley did much more than this. He was the first person from Europe to cross Africa from the east to the west.

Henry Stanley

Henry Stanley was born in Wales. When he was sixteen, he got a job as a **journalist** in America. He wrote for a newspaper and was sent to find Livingstone in Africa. The newspaper made a big story of his success.

Stanley wanted to explore more of Africa. He had read over 130 books about the country. He wanted to know more about the lakes in East Africa, and also about the Congo River in the west. Today, this river is called the Zaire River.

◀ Henry Stanley, on the right, found David Livingstone at Ujiji, a port on Lake Tanganyika. Henry Stanley was a journalist. His newspaper sent him to Africa to find David Livingstone and then to explore the country. He wrote about his travels for his newspaper.

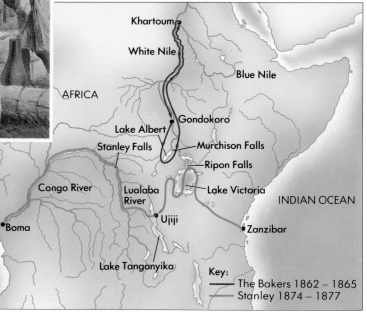

▶ This map shows the journeys of discovery made by the Bakers and Henry Stanley in the 1800's. The Bakers explored the area around Lake Albert.

Khartoum
White Nile
Blue Nile
AFRICA
Gondokoro
Lake Albert
Stanley Falls
Murchison Falls
Ripon Falls
Congo River
Lualaba River
Lake Victoria
INDIAN OCEAN
Ujiji
Boma
Zanzibar
Lake Tanganyika

Key:
— The Bakers 1862 – 1865
— Stanley 1874 – 1877

In 1874, Stanley set out from Zanzibar in East Africa. He had three friends with him. They were the Pocock brothers and a man named Frederick Barker. He also took nine tons of baggage and 356 men came along to carry it. The party even carried a wooden boat to use on the lakes. It was called the *Lady Alice*.

Island Attack

Stanley did not have an easy journey. Thieves stole some of his food and supplies. He also lost some of his men when they were attacked by native people. The explorers passed through an area where people were dying of hunger.

▼ Richard Burton and John Speke were the first Europeans to explore Lake Tanganyika. They were followed by David Livingstone and Henry Stanley.

This **famine** area was all around Lake Victoria. On the lake, there were bad storms, and they almost lost the *Lady Alice*. Once, they landed on an island, but had to escape quickly when they were attacked again. The explorers had to leave their oars behind.

Stanley and his men managed to go around the lake in fifty-seven days. They came across the waterfall known as The Stones that Speke had found before them. They renamed it the Ripon Falls.

Stanley moved south to Lake Tanganyika, which Burton and Speke had found. He sailed around it to see if this could also be a source of the Nile. Then, he found a river which he wanted to explore. It was the Lualaba, which flows to the west of the lake. Stanley planned to follow it to its mouth.

Stanley Travels West

▲ Tippu Tib was a famous Arab trader. He traded in slaves and ivory and traveled in Central Africa.

Stanley had lost two thirds of his men by the time he was ready to leave Lake Tanganyika. Some had died or had been killed. Others had run away. They were afraid that Stanley would lead them into even greater dangers. Stanley now climbed up into mountains on the west of Lake Tanganyika.

In the mountains, Stanley met a rich Arab who had made his money from the slave trade. He was the most feared man in Central Africa. He was named Tippu Tib. He was a tall man with a big black beard. Stanley needed Tippu Tib's help. Stanley said he would pay him a lot of money if he would travel with him for sixty days. For this money, Tippu Tib had to go to any place Stanley chose. In spite of the dangers, Tippu Tib agreed to do what Stanley wanted. It was too much money for him to turn down.

Into the Jungle

Stanley chose to go north. The area to the north was said to be full of snakes and cruel, warlike people. Tippu Tib had never been there before. He thought the area was too dangerous.

At first, the main problem was the thick, wet jungle. Stanley and the men had to cut their way through the jungle. Progress was very slow. Tippu Tib said that the hot, damp air was killing his people. He would go no farther. He took his money and left Stanley and his men to go on alone.

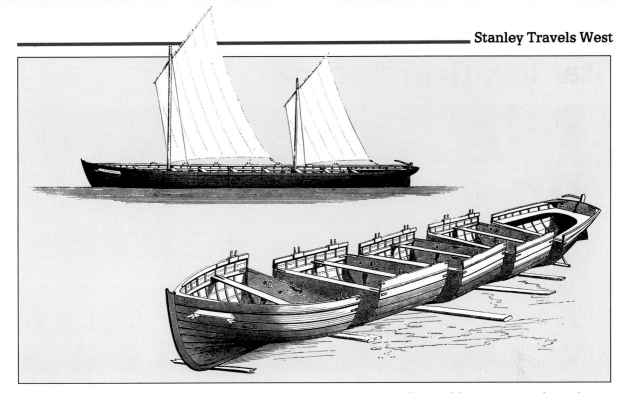

▲ The *Lady Alice* could be divided into five pieces. This made it easier to carry it overland or around rapids and waterfalls.

▼ Henry Stanley could not continue down the river because of the cataracts. He and his party had to cut their way through the jungle.

Down the River

Stanley traveled on by river. He had carried the *Lady Alice* in parts, or **sections**, all this way. Now, he rebuilt the boat and set off on the Lualaba River. He thought this river might join the Congo River.

All the way along the river, they were attacked by people in canoes. Their drums could be heard on the river banks. Stanley and his men reached a place where the water rushed down a steep cliff. There were seven of these **cataracts**. These falls are now called the Stanley Falls. The explorers had to carry their boat around the falls. All the time, they were under attack from people on the river bank.

The Death of Pocock

▲ Henry Stanley set off with Tippu Tib and about 1,000 people on his journey down the Congo River. They were often attacked by people who lived along the river banks.

The river became wider. In some places, it was almost four miles across. Yet the attacks continued. Stanley wrote that to go from the right bank to the left was "like jumping from the frying pan into the fire." The attacks came from both banks of the river. Once, over fifty large war canoes came to attack them. Stanley and his men only just got away from them in time.

The men paddled and pulled the boat for 1,000 miles down the river. Then, they reached a large open pool. All around were white cliffs. Frank Pocock said that they looked like the white cliffs of Dover back in Britain. He dreamed that they would soon be home.

Pocock had traveled with Stanley for 6,875 miles from Zanzibar. He was now very sick. He could not walk at all. All he could do was crawl. He died very soon after. He drowned in some rapids because he was too weak to save himself. Stanley wept for his "dear lost friend."

The Congo River

Other people in Stanley's party became restless. They were hungry, tired, and far from home. They were also afraid. Many of their friends had already died. Stanley made them go on.

▼ Frank Pocock was very weak from sickness when he and Henry Stanley were sailing down the Congo River. When they came to a series of rapids, the boat Pocock was traveling in overturned and he was drowned.

▲ Stanley used the *Lady Alice* for much of his journey down the Congo River.

Rapids blocked their way again. Stanley himself almost drowned. They had to drag the *Lady Alice* overland. The porters were so tired that Stanley made a track with wooden rollers for the boat. For this, he had to cut a pathway five yards wide through the trees. It took many days to move a mile. In one day, eight men were lost in accidents.

At last, they found a more friendly chief. Stanley asked him the name of the river. He said, "Ikuta ya Kongo." Stanley had found the Congo River at last.

The West Coast

Stanley now decided to go to a trading post called Boma, which was on the coast. He was short of food, so he sent a message on ahead of him. He was sent food, which saved him and his porters.

Stanley reached the west coast of Africa 999 days after leaving Zanzibar on the east coast. His hair was almost white! Stanley, or the "breaker of rocks," as the local people named him, had made a famous journey.

The President Explorer

▲ Theodore Roosevelt with a jaguar he shot in Brazil. Roosevelt was President from 1901 to 1909.

Today, all of the longest rivers of the world have been explored. Some fast-flowing streams and rivers in faraway, or **remote**, places have not been followed from source to mouth. People still want to explore these rivers.

Theodore Roosevelt was very famous before he became an explorer. He had been President of the United States. He had always enjoyed being outdoors, and had won many prizes for hunting.

In 1913, when Roosevelt was fifty-three, he decided to take his son Kermit on a great adventure. They wanted to trace the course of a river in South America called the Duvido River, or "the river of doubt." This river flows through Brazil, and it was not on any maps at that time. Its source had been found in 1909, but the only thing that was known was that the river flowed north.

Exploring the River

Roosevelt went with some army officers from Brazil, a doctor, and some native people. They began their journey in Paraguay, and went with seven canoes up the Paraguay River to the high, flat Mato Grosso area. The rainy season had begun, and the rivers ran swiftly. When they reached the Duvido River, they had to carry their canoes past the rapids. They were attacked by insects all the time. Roosevelt had to wear gloves and a hat with netting to protect him from insect bites. By this time, three of their canoes had been lost or broken. They shot monkeys and parrots for food. The climate was so hot and sticky that their clothes were always dripping wet.

Roosevelt and his men decided to go down the rapids in their canoes. It would take too long to drag them around the steep cliffs and through the jungles. At first, all went well. Then, there was a terrible accident. Kermit and two of the men lost control of their canoe in the rapids. The canoe overturned, and one of them was killed. Kermit was lucky to escape. He grabbed a low branch and just managed to pull himself on to the bank of the river.

The River Gets a New Name

Their progress was slow. The men had only come seventy-five miles in three weeks. Both Roosevelt and Kermit had the fever, and the other people in the party were weak from sickness and hunger. At last, they came to a rubber tree farm, or **plantation**. The worst part

▲ Captain Kermit Roosevelt photographed on the Duvido River.

of the journey was over. They reached Manaus fifteen days later. Theodore Roosevelt had put the river on the map. It is now called the Theodore Roosevelt River in his honor.

Exploring Alone

Christina Dodwell is a British woman who got her first taste for adventure in Africa. In 1975, she went with three others in a jeep across the Sahara Desert. When they arrived in West Africa, two of the people stole the jeep. Christina and her friend did not give up. They bought some horses and spent the next year riding through West Africa. They also paddled a canoe for over 1,000 miles through the hot, wet **tropical rain forests**. After this, Christina continued alone for another 625 miles.

Christina began to enjoy being a lone explorer. Later, she traveled by camel through the East African Rift Valley into Ethiopia. The people there thought she was a spy.

Christina went back to Britain. She wanted to plan a trip to somewhere even more remote. She loved the thrill and risk of exploring by herself. She chose Papua New Guinea, a country north of Australia. There were people there who still lived like people from the Stone Age. Papua New Guinea has been called "the last unknown."

Adventures in the Highlands

Christina traveled to the highland area of Papua New Guinea. She rode for 1,000 miles on horseback through the mountains. She lived through a minor **earthquake**, and once she saw a battle with bows and arrows. In Africa, she had learned to ride through swamps and over rotten bridges. She was also used to riding through narrow mountain paths, or **ravines**. She was so good at riding that she won a prize in a local "bucking-bronco" contest.

▼ One of the problems traveling by truck is that it can get stuck in the mud! Often, Christina Dodwell found it was better to travel by horse or canoe in parts of Papua New Guinea.

▶ Christina Dodwell at Kraimbit. The people are getting ready for a festival.

Christina then spent four months paddling a canoe on remote parts of the Sepik River. Children ran away when they saw her. They had never seen a European woman before. Their parents were not afraid of her, but curious and friendly. They gave her a mixture made from a grain called sago to eat. It was a local food which looked like grey jellyfish! It did not taste very good, but it was very healthy to eat.

Christina made her way along the river. The climate was hot and sticky, and she was often very uncomfortable. She said the river smelled of fresh mud mixed with flower perfume.

Mama Dodwell

Some of the native people thought their families from the past, or **ancestors**, had pale skins like Christina. They thought Christina must be an ancestor, and even called her "Mama Dodwell." Other people called her "Sepik woman" because they were amazed to see her in her canoe on the river. They thought she was very brave to travel alone.

The journeys of Christina Dodwell show that even today there are great adventures to be found for people with courage and spirit.

▼ The area Christina Dodwell traveled through in Papua New Guinea.

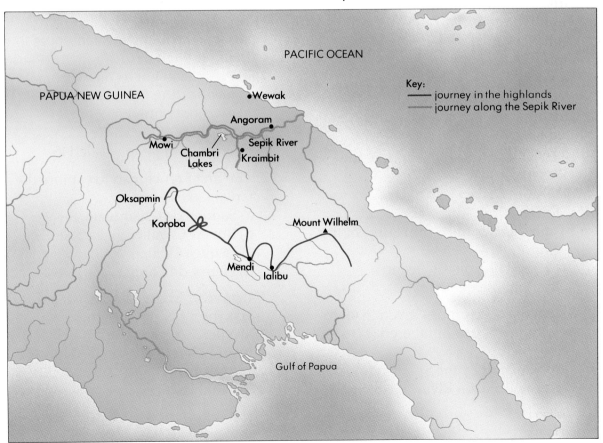

Quiz

How much can you remember about this book? Try this quiz. Use your glossary and index to help you find the answers.

1. Here are some scrambled names of famous river explorers. Unscramble them to find out who they are.
   a) PRAK, b) PEKES, c) SLAYNET,
   d) RITECAR, e) MACHPLAIN,
   f) LANARELO, g) LEASLAL, h) CRUBE

2. a) Which river flows into the Gulf of Mexico?
   b) Which river joins with the Negro?
   c) Which river has its source in Ethiopia?
   d) Which river has a President's name?

3. Put the following events in the order that they took place.
   a) A British woman explores the Sepik River.
   b) La Salle travels the length of the Mississippi River.
   c) Jacques Cartier sets out to look for the Northwest-Passage.
   d) James Bruce finds the source of the Blue Nile.
   e) Richard Burton is killed in a hunting accident.

4. Match the descriptions given in (a) to (f) with the words numbered (1) to (6) below them.
   a) A boat built by the Spanish to sail on the Amazon River

b) A companion of John Speke
c) A river in Papua New Guinea
d) A female explorer in Africa
e) A grassy area in Africa
f) A boat used by Henry Stanley

1) Florence Baker
2) *Lady Alice*
3) savanna
4) Sepik
5) James Grant
6) *Victoria*

5. Where would you be if you were in or on the following?
   a) A river "black as ink"
   b) A route from the North Atlantic Ocean to the Pacific Ocean
   c) The place where the Blue Nile joins the White Nile

6. Complete the following sentences with (a), (b), (c), or (d).
   1) The Amazon got its name from
      a) meat-eating fish.
      b) warrior women.
      c) the color of the water.
      d) what local people called it.

   2) The first Frenchman to explore the Great Lakes was
      a) Samuel de Champlain.
      b) Robert Cavalier de La Salle.
      c) Jacques Cartier.
      d) Henry de Tonty.

   3) One river Mungo Park traveled on was the
      a) Nile.
      b) St. Lawrence.
      c) Amazon.
      d) Gambia.

4) A group of people with camels is called a
   a) camel car.
   b) fleet.
   c) caravan.
   d) regiment.

5) Mutesa was
   a) a mountain.
   b) a river.
   c) a chief in Africa.
   d) a Huron leader.

6) Gondokoro is on the river
   a) Niger.
   b) Nile.
   c) Senegal.
   d) Congo.

7. How many river explorers can you find with names beginning with C, S or B?

8. Who or what
   a) went down the Napo River?
   b) named the city of Montreal?
   c) was called a "winged canoe?"
   d) traveled in the Mato Grosso area?
   e) was known as "Mama" by local people?

9. Which one does not belong in each group?
   a) Amazon, Nile, St. Lawrence, Cubagua
   b) Bruce, Orellana, La Salle, Ras Mikael
   c) Khartoum, Nile, Montreal, Cairo

10. Are these statements True or False?
    a) Robert Cavalier de La Salle was a fur trader.
    b) Mungo Park crossed the Sahara Desert.
    c) The Nile River flows through Egypt.
    d) James Bruce was the first European to see the source of the Blue Nile.
    e) The Bakers found Lake Albert.

Answers

1. a) PARK b) SPEKE c) STANLEY d) CARTIER e) CHAMPLAIN f) ORELLANA g) LA SALLE h) BRUCE

2. (a) Mississippi, (b) Amazon, (c) Blue Nile (d) Theodore Roosevelt

3. (c), (b), (d), (e), (a)

4. (a) 6, (b) 5, (c) 4, (d) 1, (e) 3, (f) 2

5. (a) Negro River, (b) Northwest Passage (c) Khartoum

6. 1 (b), 2 (a), 3 (d), 4 (c), 5 (c), 6 (b)

7. Cartier, Champlain, Carvajal, Stanley, La Salle, Speke, Baker, Bruce, Brulé, Burton, Barker

8. (a) Orellana, (b) Cartier, (c) *the Griffon*, (d) Roosevelt, (e) Christina Dodwell

9. (a) Cubagua (b) Ras Mikael, (c) Nile

10. (a) true, (b) false, (c) true, (d) false, (e) true

45

Glossary

ancestor: a relative who lived and died a long time ago.

bank: a raised slope of earth along the edge of a river, a lake, or a road.

blowpipe: a long straight tube through which darts or pellets can be blown.

bushland: describes wild, uncultivated land where few people live. Areas of bushland are found in Africa and Australia.

caravan: a group of people and their camels traveling across the desert.

cataract: a large area where water falls steeply over rocks.

channel: a pathway along which something can go, like water along the bed of a river.

cinnamon: a spice made from the yellowish-brown bark of the evergreen cinnamon tree. The cinnamon tree used to grow wild in Sri Lanka.

compass: an instrument that is used to find direction. It contains a needle which points North. The four points of the compass are North, South, East, and West.

continent: a large mass of land, usually including many countries. The earth is divided into seven continents.

crew: the group of people who work together on a ship or plane.

current: the flow of water within a sea, lake, or river.

earthquake: a sudden shaking of the land due to movements in the layers of rock under the earth's surface.

East: the countries of Asia. Asia was often called the East because travelers came from Europe and journeyed eastwards to get there.

expedition: an organized journey which is made for a special purpose. Explorers went on expeditions to find out about new lands.

famine: a time when there is little or no food in a country or region because of a disaster like a bad drought.

fleet: a number of ships sailing together, usually under one commander.

fort: a building which has strong walls so that the people inside can defend themselves against an enemy.

heir: the person who will be given, by law, a title, money, or property when the present owner dies.

herb: any plant used for medicine or to add flavor in cooking.

hostile: unfriendly.

interior: the inside of something. The interior is the part of a country that is far from the sea.

journalist: someone who writes for a newspaper or a magazine.

junction: a place where things such as rivers, roads, or railway lines join.

limpid: describes something that can easily be seen through. Water is often described as limpid when it is clear and still.

missionary: a person sent by a religious group to tell other people about their faith or beliefs.

moccasin: a soft leather shoe usually made of deerskin.

mouth: the part of a river where it flows into a sea or lake.

mutiny: to refuse to obey the people in charge. When sailors or soldiers attack their officers, it is called a mutiny.

Northwest Passage: a route from the Atlantic Ocean to the Pacific Ocean across the top of North America.

Orient: another word for Asia, especially China or Japan.

party: a group of people working or taking part in an activity together.

plague: a disease spread by rats. Plague can be caught easily and it can kill many people.

plantation: a large area of land where one type of plant or tree is grown. Coffee, rubber, and tea are grown on plantations.

quadrant: an instrument used to measure the height of the stars. Sailors used a quadrant to steer their ships in the right direction.

rapid: a part of the river where the water flows very fast over rocks. The water is usually shallow so the rocks make it very rough to sail over.

ravine: a deep narrow valley made by fast running water.

reach: a stage of a river. The stage near the beginning of a river is called the upper reach.

reed: a stalk of a tall, thin grass-like plant found by the water or in water. A reed is hollow inside.

remote: describes something which is far-away, or distant. A remote island is a long way from other lands.

route: the way to get from one place to another. Routes are shown on maps and plans.

rudder: a hinged, flat piece of wood, or metal, used to steer boats, planes, or spacecraft.

savanna: a hot, dry grassland with few trees in Africa.

section: a part or piece of something.

site: the ground on which a town or building is to be built, is standing, or has stood.

slave trader: a person who bought or sold people as slaves.

source: the place where something begins. The source of a river can be a spring or a lake.

supplies: food, fuel, or equipment needed for an expedition or a trip.

tropical rain forest: a very hot, damp forest found in the regions close to the equator. Tropical forests have tall trees and plants which grow very close together.

warehouse: a building in which goods are stored.

waterfall: a cliff in a river bed over which the water falls straight down.

Index